— Order Log —

BUSINESS NAME:
_____

CONTACT:
_____

EMAIL:
_____

Index

Order No.	Customer Name	Order No.	Customer Name	Order No.	Customer Name

Index

Order No.	Customer Name	Order No.	Customer Name	Order No.	Customer Name

ORDER NO.:	NAME:		DATE:	
	CONTACT:		EMAIL:	
	ADDRESS:			

ITEM NO.	ITEM DESCRIPTION	QTY.	PRICE

NOTES:		SUBTOTAL	
		SHIPPING	
		DISCOUNT	
		TOTAL	

PAYMENT METHOD: DATE SHIPPED:

PAYMENT DATE: SHIPPING SERVICE:

PROCESS: STARTED   DONE   CANCELED   TRACKING NO.:

ORDER NO.:	NAME:		DATE:	
	CONTACT:		EMAIL:	
	ADDRESS:			

ITEM NO.	ITEM DESCRIPTION	QTY.	PRICE

NOTES:		SUBTOTAL	
		SHIPPING	
		DISCOUNT	
		TOTAL	

PAYMENT METHOD: DATE SHIPPED:

PAYMENT DATE: SHIPPING SERVICE:

PROCESS: STARTED   DONE   CANCELED   TRACKING NO.:

ORDER NO.:	NAME:		DATE:	
	CONTACT:		EMAIL:	
	ADDRESS:			

ITEM NO.	ITEM DESCRIPTION	QTY.	PRICE

NOTES:		
	SUBTOTAL	
	SHIPPING	
	DISCOUNT	
	TOTAL	

PAYMENT METHOD: DATE SHIPPED:

PAYMENT DATE: SHIPPING SERVICE:

PROCESS: STARTED   DONE   CANCELED   TRACKING NO.:

ORDER NO.:	NAME:		DATE:	
	CONTACT:		EMAIL:	
	ADDRESS:			

ITEM NO.	ITEM DESCRIPTION	QTY.	PRICE

NOTES:		
	SUBTOTAL	
	SHIPPING	
	DISCOUNT	
	TOTAL	

PAYMENT METHOD: DATE SHIPPED:

PAYMENT DATE: SHIPPING SERVICE:

PROCESS: STARTED   DONE   CANCELED   TRACKING NO.:

ORDER NO.:	NAME:			DATE:	
	CONTACT:			EMAIL:	
	ADDRESS:				

ITEM NO.	ITEM DESCRIPTION	QTY.	PRICE

NOTES:		SUBTOTAL	
		SHIPPING	
		DISCOUNT	
		TOTAL	

PAYMENT METHOD: DATE SHIPPED:

PAYMENT DATE: SHIPPING SERVICE:

PROCESS: STARTED   DONE   CANCELED   TRACKING NO.:

ORDER NO.:	NAME:			DATE:	
	CONTACT:			EMAIL:	
	ADDRESS:				

ITEM NO.	ITEM DESCRIPTION	QTY.	PRICE

NOTES:		SUBTOTAL	
		SHIPPING	
		DISCOUNT	
		TOTAL	

PAYMENT METHOD: DATE SHIPPED:

PAYMENT DATE: SHIPPING SERVICE:

PROCESS: STARTED   DONE   CANCELED   TRACKING NO.:

ORDER NO.:	NAME:		DATE:	
	CONTACT:		EMAIL:	
	ADDRESS:			

ITEM NO.	ITEM DESCRIPTION	QTY.	PRICE

NOTES:		
	SUBTOTAL	
	SHIPPING	
	DISCOUNT	
	TOTAL	

PAYMENT METHOD: DATE SHIPPED:

PAYMENT DATE: SHIPPING SERVICE:

PROCESS: STARTED   D O N E   CANCELED   TRACKING NO.:

ORDER NO.:	NAME:		DATE:	
	CONTACT:		EMAIL:	
	ADDRESS:			

ITEM NO.	ITEM DESCRIPTION	QTY.	PRICE

NOTES:		
	SUBTOTAL	
	SHIPPING	
	DISCOUNT	
	TOTAL	

PAYMENT METHOD: DATE SHIPPED:

PAYMENT DATE: SHIPPING SERVICE:

PROCESS: STARTED   D O N E   CANCELED   TRACKING NO.:

ORDER NO.:	NAME:		DATE:	
	CONTACT:		EMAIL:	
	ADDRESS:			

ITEM NO.	ITEM DESCRIPTION	QTY.	PRICE

NOTES:		
	SUBTOTAL	
	SHIPPING	
	DISCOUNT	
	TOTAL	

PAYMENT METHOD: DATE SHIPPED:

PAYMENT DATE: SHIPPING SERVICE:

PROCESS: STARTED   DONE   CANCELED   TRACKING NO.:

ORDER NO.:	NAME:		DATE:	
	CONTACT:		EMAIL:	
	ADDRESS:			

ITEM NO.	ITEM DESCRIPTION	QTY.	PRICE

NOTES:		
	SUBTOTAL	
	SHIPPING	
	DISCOUNT	
	TOTAL	

PAYMENT METHOD: DATE SHIPPED:

PAYMENT DATE: SHIPPING SERVICE:

PROCESS: STARTED   DONE   CANCELED   TRACKING NO.:

ORDER NO.:	NAME:		DATE:	
	CONTACT:		EMAIL:	
	ADDRESS:			

ITEM NO.	ITEM DESCRIPTION	QTY.	PRICE

NOTES:		
	SUBTOTAL	
	SHIPPING	
	DISCOUNT	
	TOTAL	

PAYMENT METHOD: DATE SHIPPED:

PAYMENT DATE: SHIPPING SERVICE:

PROCESS: STARTED   DONE   CANCELED   TRACKING NO.:

ORDER NO.:	NAME:		DATE:	
	CONTACT:		EMAIL:	
	ADDRESS:			

ITEM NO.	ITEM DESCRIPTION	QTY.	PRICE

NOTES:		
	SUBTOTAL	
	SHIPPING	
	DISCOUNT	
	TOTAL	

PAYMENT METHOD: DATE SHIPPED:

PAYMENT DATE: SHIPPING SERVICE:

PROCESS: STARTED   DONE   CANCELED   TRACKING NO.:

ORDER NO.:	NAME:		DATE:	
	CONTACT:		EMAIL:	
	ADDRESS:			

ITEM NO.	ITEM DESCRIPTION	QTY.	PRICE

NOTES:			
		SUBTOTAL	
		SHIPPING	
		DISCOUNT	
		TOTAL	

PAYMENT METHOD: DATE SHIPPED:

PAYMENT DATE: SHIPPING SERVICE:

PROCESS: STARTED   DONE   CANCELED   TRACKING NO.:

ORDER NO.:	NAME:		DATE:	
	CONTACT:		EMAIL:	
	ADDRESS:			

ITEM NO.	ITEM DESCRIPTION	QTY.	PRICE

NOTES:			
		SUBTOTAL	
		SHIPPING	
		DISCOUNT	
		TOTAL	

PAYMENT METHOD: DATE SHIPPED:

PAYMENT DATE: SHIPPING SERVICE:

PROCESS: STARTED   DONE   CANCELED   TRACKING NO.:

ORDER NO.:	NAME:		DATE:	
	CONTACT:		EMAIL:	
	ADDRESS:			

ITEM NO.	ITEM DESCRIPTION	QTY.	PRICE

NOTES:		
	SUBTOTAL	
	SHIPPING	
	DISCOUNT	
	TOTAL	

PAYMENT METHOD: DATE SHIPPED:

PAYMENT DATE: SHIPPING SERVICE:

PROCESS: STARTED   DONE   CANCELED   TRACKING NO.:

ORDER NO.:	NAME:		DATE:	
	CONTACT:		EMAIL:	
	ADDRESS:			

ITEM NO.	ITEM DESCRIPTION	QTY.	PRICE

NOTES:		
	SUBTOTAL	
	SHIPPING	
	DISCOUNT	
	TOTAL	

PAYMENT METHOD: DATE SHIPPED:

PAYMENT DATE: SHIPPING SERVICE:

PROCESS: STARTED   DONE   CANCELED   TRACKING NO.:

ORDER NO.:	NAME:		DATE:	
	CONTACT:		EMAIL:	
	ADDRESS:			

ITEM NO.	ITEM DESCRIPTION	QTY.	PRICE

NOTES:			
	SUBTOTAL	
	SHIPPING	
	DISCOUNT	
	TOTAL	

PAYMENT METHOD: DATE SHIPPED:

PAYMENT DATE: SHIPPING SERVICE:

PROCESS: STARTED   DONE   CANCELED   TRACKING NO.:

ORDER NO.:	NAME:		DATE:	
	CONTACT:		EMAIL:	
	ADDRESS:			

ITEM NO.	ITEM DESCRIPTION	QTY.	PRICE

NOTES:			
	SUBTOTAL	
	SHIPPING	
	DISCOUNT	
	TOTAL	

PAYMENT METHOD: DATE SHIPPED:

PAYMENT DATE: SHIPPING SERVICE:

PROCESS: STARTED   DONE   CANCELED   TRACKING NO.:

ORDER NO.:	NAME:		DATE:	
	CONTACT:		EMAIL:	
	ADDRESS:			

ITEM NO.	ITEM DESCRIPTION	QTY.	PRICE

NOTES:		
	SUBTOTAL	
	SHIPPING	
	DISCOUNT	
	TOTAL	

PAYMENT METHOD: DATE SHIPPED:

PAYMENT DATE: SHIPPING SERVICE:

PROCESS: STARTED   DONE   CANCELED   TRACKING NO.:

ORDER NO.:	NAME:		DATE:	
	CONTACT:		EMAIL:	
	ADDRESS:			

ITEM NO.	ITEM DESCRIPTION	QTY.	PRICE

NOTES:		
	SUBTOTAL	
	SHIPPING	
	DISCOUNT	
	TOTAL	

PAYMENT METHOD: DATE SHIPPED:

PAYMENT DATE: SHIPPING SERVICE:

PROCESS: STARTED   DONE   CANCELED   TRACKING NO.:

ORDER NO.:	NAME:		DATE:	
	CONTACT:		EMAIL:	
	ADDRESS:			

ITEM NO.	ITEM DESCRIPTION	QTY.	PRICE

NOTES:		
	SUBTOTAL	
	SHIPPING	
	DISCOUNT	
	TOTAL	

PAYMENT METHOD: DATE SHIPPED:

PAYMENT DATE: SHIPPING SERVICE:

PROCESS: STARTED DONE CANCELED TRACKING NO.:

ORDER NO.:	NAME:		DATE:	
	CONTACT:		EMAIL:	
	ADDRESS:			

ITEM NO.	ITEM DESCRIPTION	QTY.	PRICE

NOTES:		
	SUBTOTAL	
	SHIPPING	
	DISCOUNT	
	TOTAL	

PAYMENT METHOD: DATE SHIPPED:

PAYMENT DATE: SHIPPING SERVICE:

PROCESS: STARTED DONE CANCELED TRACKING NO.:

ORDER NO.:	NAME:		DATE:	
	CONTACT:		EMAIL:	
	ADDRESS:			

ITEM NO.	ITEM DESCRIPTION	QTY.	PRICE

NOTES:	SUBTOTAL	
	SHIPPING	
	DISCOUNT	
	TOTAL	

PAYMENT METHOD: DATE SHIPPED:

PAYMENT DATE: SHIPPING SERVICE:

PROCESS: STARTED DONE CANCELED TRACKING NO.:

ORDER NO.:	NAME:		DATE:	
	CONTACT:		EMAIL:	
	ADDRESS:			

ITEM NO.	ITEM DESCRIPTION	QTY.	PRICE

NOTES:	SUBTOTAL	
	SHIPPING	
	DISCOUNT	
	TOTAL	

PAYMENT METHOD: DATE SHIPPED:

PAYMENT DATE: SHIPPING SERVICE:

PROCESS: STARTED DONE CANCELED TRACKING NO.:

ORDER NO.:	NAME:		DATE:	
	CONTACT:		EMAIL:	
	ADDRESS:			

ITEM NO.	ITEM DESCRIPTION	QTY.	PRICE

NOTES:			
		SUBTOTAL	
		SHIPPING	
		DISCOUNT	
		TOTAL	

PAYMENT METHOD: DATE SHIPPED:

PAYMENT DATE: SHIPPING SERVICE:

PROCESS: STARTED   DONE   CANCELED   TRACKING NO.:

ORDER NO.:	NAME:		DATE:	
	CONTACT:		EMAIL:	
	ADDRESS:			

ITEM NO.	ITEM DESCRIPTION	QTY.	PRICE

NOTES:			
		SUBTOTAL	
		SHIPPING	
		DISCOUNT	
		TOTAL	

PAYMENT METHOD: DATE SHIPPED:

PAYMENT DATE: SHIPPING SERVICE:

PROCESS: STARTED   DONE   CANCELED   TRACKING NO.:

ORDER NO.:	NAME:		DATE:	
	CONTACT:		EMAIL:	
	ADDRESS:			

ITEM NO.	ITEM DESCRIPTION	QTY.	PRICE

NOTES:		
	SUBTOTAL	
	SHIPPING	
	DISCOUNT	
	TOTAL	

PAYMENT METHOD: DATE SHIPPED:

PAYMENT DATE: SHIPPING SERVICE:

PROCESS: STARTED   DONE   CANCELED   TRACKING NO.:

ORDER NO.:	NAME:		DATE:	
	CONTACT:		EMAIL:	
	ADDRESS:			

ITEM NO.	ITEM DESCRIPTION	QTY.	PRICE

NOTES:		
	SUBTOTAL	
	SHIPPING	
	DISCOUNT	
	TOTAL	

PAYMENT METHOD: DATE SHIPPED:

PAYMENT DATE: SHIPPING SERVICE:

PROCESS: STARTED   DONE   CANCELED   TRACKING NO.:

ORDER NO.:	NAME:		DATE:	
	CONTACT:		EMAIL:	
	ADDRESS:			

ITEM NO.	ITEM DESCRIPTION	QTY.	PRICE

NOTES:		
	SUBTOTAL	
	SHIPPING	
	DISCOUNT	
	TOTAL	

PAYMENT METHOD: DATE SHIPPED:

PAYMENT DATE: SHIPPING SERVICE:

PROCESS: STARTED   DONE   CANCELED   TRACKING NO.:

ORDER NO.:	NAME:		DATE:	
	CONTACT:		EMAIL:	
	ADDRESS:			

ITEM NO.	ITEM DESCRIPTION	QTY.	PRICE

NOTES:		
	SUBTOTAL	
	SHIPPING	
	DISCOUNT	
	TOTAL	

PAYMENT METHOD: DATE SHIPPED:

PAYMENT DATE: SHIPPING SERVICE:

PROCESS: STARTED   DONE   CANCELED   TRACKING NO.:

ORDER NO.:	NAME:		DATE:	
	CONTACT:		EMAIL:	
	ADDRESS:			

ITEM NO.	ITEM DESCRIPTION	QTY.	PRICE

NOTES:			
	SUBTOTAL	
	SHIPPING	
	DISCOUNT	
	TOTAL	

PAYMENT METHOD: DATE SHIPPED:

PAYMENT DATE: SHIPPING SERVICE:

PROCESS: STARTED   DONE   CANCELED   TRACKING NO.:

ORDER NO.:	NAME:		DATE:	
	CONTACT:		EMAIL:	
	ADDRESS:			

ITEM NO.	ITEM DESCRIPTION	QTY.	PRICE

NOTES:			
	SUBTOTAL	
	SHIPPING	
	DISCOUNT	
	TOTAL	

PAYMENT METHOD: DATE SHIPPED:

PAYMENT DATE: SHIPPING SERVICE:

PROCESS: STARTED   DONE   CANCELED   TRACKING NO.:

ORDER NO.:	NAME:		DATE:	
	CONTACT:		EMAIL:	
	ADDRESS:			

ITEM NO.	ITEM DESCRIPTION	QTY.	PRICE

NOTES:		
	SUBTOTAL	
	SHIPPING	
	DISCOUNT	
	TOTAL	

PAYMENT METHOD: DATE SHIPPED:

PAYMENT DATE: SHIPPING SERVICE:

PROCESS: ☐ STARTED ☐ DONE ☐ CANCELED TRACKING NO.:

ORDER NO.:	NAME:		DATE:	
	CONTACT:		EMAIL:	
	ADDRESS:			

ITEM NO.	ITEM DESCRIPTION	QTY.	PRICE

NOTES:		
	SUBTOTAL	
	SHIPPING	
	DISCOUNT	
	TOTAL	

PAYMENT METHOD: DATE SHIPPED:

PAYMENT DATE: SHIPPING SERVICE:

PROCESS: ☐ STARTED ☐ DONE ☐ CANCELED TRACKING NO.:

ORDER NO.:	NAME:		DATE:	
	CONTACT:		EMAIL:	
	ADDRESS:			

ITEM NO.	ITEM DESCRIPTION	QTY.	PRICE

NOTES:		
	SUBTOTAL	
	SHIPPING	
	DISCOUNT	
	TOTAL	

PAYMENT METHOD: DATE SHIPPED:

PAYMENT DATE: SHIPPING SERVICE:

PROCESS: STARTED   DONE   CANCELED   TRACKING NO.:

ORDER NO.:	NAME:		DATE:	
	CONTACT:		EMAIL:	
	ADDRESS:			

ITEM NO.	ITEM DESCRIPTION	QTY.	PRICE

NOTES:		
	SUBTOTAL	
	SHIPPING	
	DISCOUNT	
	TOTAL	

PAYMENT METHOD: DATE SHIPPED:

PAYMENT DATE: SHIPPING SERVICE:

PROCESS: STARTED   DONE   CANCELED   TRACKING NO.:

ORDER NO.:	NAME:		DATE:	
	CONTACT:		EMAIL:	
	ADDRESS:			

ITEM NO.	ITEM DESCRIPTION	QTY.	PRICE

NOTES:		
	SUBTOTAL	
	SHIPPING	
	DISCOUNT	
	TOTAL	

PAYMENT METHOD: DATE SHIPPED:

PAYMENT DATE: SHIPPING SERVICE:

PROCESS: STARTED   DONE   CANCELED   TRACKING NO.:

ORDER NO.:	NAME:		DATE:	
	CONTACT:		EMAIL:	
	ADDRESS:			

ITEM NO.	ITEM DESCRIPTION	QTY.	PRICE

NOTES:		
	SUBTOTAL	
	SHIPPING	
	DISCOUNT	
	TOTAL	

PAYMENT METHOD: DATE SHIPPED:

PAYMENT DATE: SHIPPING SERVICE:

PROCESS: STARTED   DONE   CANCELED   TRACKING NO.:

ORDER NO.:	NAME:		DATE:	
	CONTACT:		EMAIL:	
	ADDRESS:			

ITEM NO.	ITEM DESCRIPTION	QTY.	PRICE

NOTES:		
	SUBTOTAL	
	SHIPPING	
	DISCOUNT	
	TOTAL	

PAYMENT METHOD: DATE SHIPPED:

PAYMENT DATE: SHIPPING SERVICE:

PROCESS: STARTED   DONE   CANCELED   TRACKING NO.:

ORDER NO.:	NAME:		DATE:	
	CONTACT:		EMAIL:	
	ADDRESS:			

ITEM NO.	ITEM DESCRIPTION	QTY.	PRICE

NOTES:		
	SUBTOTAL	
	SHIPPING	
	DISCOUNT	
	TOTAL	

PAYMENT METHOD: DATE SHIPPED:

PAYMENT DATE: SHIPPING SERVICE:

PROCESS: STARTED   DONE   CANCELED   TRACKING NO.:

ORDER NO.:	NAME:		DATE:	
	CONTACT:		EMAIL:	
	ADDRESS:			

ITEM NO.	ITEM DESCRIPTION	QTY.	PRICE

NOTES:		SUBTOTAL	
		SHIPPING	
		DISCOUNT	
		TOTAL	

PAYMENT METHOD: DATE SHIPPED:

PAYMENT DATE: SHIPPING SERVICE:

PROCESS: STARTED   DONE   CANCELED   TRACKING NO.:

ORDER NO.:	NAME:		DATE:	
	CONTACT:		EMAIL:	
	ADDRESS:			

ITEM NO.	ITEM DESCRIPTION	QTY.	PRICE

NOTES:		SUBTOTAL	
		SHIPPING	
		DISCOUNT	
		TOTAL	

PAYMENT METHOD: DATE SHIPPED:

PAYMENT DATE: SHIPPING SERVICE:

PROCESS: STARTED   DONE   CANCELED   TRACKING NO.:

ORDER NO.:	NAME:		DATE:	
	CONTACT:		EMAIL:	
	ADDRESS:			

ITEM NO.	ITEM DESCRIPTION	QTY.	PRICE

NOTES:		
	SUBTOTAL	
	SHIPPING	
	DISCOUNT	
	TOTAL	

PAYMENT METHOD: DATE SHIPPED:

PAYMENT DATE: SHIPPING SERVICE:

PROCESS: STARTED   DONE   CANCELED   TRACKING NO.:

ORDER NO.:	NAME:		DATE:	
	CONTACT:		EMAIL:	
	ADDRESS:			

ITEM NO.	ITEM DESCRIPTION	QTY.	PRICE

NOTES:		
	SUBTOTAL	
	SHIPPING	
	DISCOUNT	
	TOTAL	

PAYMENT METHOD: DATE SHIPPED:

PAYMENT DATE: SHIPPING SERVICE:

PROCESS: STARTED   DONE   CANCELED   TRACKING NO.:

ORDER NO.:	NAME:		DATE:	
	CONTACT:		EMAIL:	
	ADDRESS:			

ITEM NO.	ITEM DESCRIPTION	QTY.	PRICE

NOTES:			SUBTOTAL	
			SHIPPING	
			DISCOUNT	
			TOTAL	

PAYMENT METHOD: DATE SHIPPED:

PAYMENT DATE: SHIPPING SERVICE:

PROCESS: STARTED   DONE   CANCELED   TRACKING NO.:

ORDER NO.:	NAME:		DATE:	
	CONTACT:		EMAIL:	
	ADDRESS:			

ITEM NO.	ITEM DESCRIPTION	QTY.	PRICE

NOTES:			SUBTOTAL	
			SHIPPING	
			DISCOUNT	
			TOTAL	

PAYMENT METHOD: DATE SHIPPED:

PAYMENT DATE: SHIPPING SERVICE:

PROCESS: STARTED   DONE   CANCELED   TRACKING NO.:

ORDER NO.:	NAME:		DATE:	
	CONTACT:		EMAIL:	
	ADDRESS:			

ITEM NO.	ITEM DESCRIPTION	QTY.	PRICE

NOTES:		SUBTOTAL	
		SHIPPING	
		DISCOUNT	
		TOTAL	

PAYMENT METHOD: DATE SHIPPED:

PAYMENT DATE: SHIPPING SERVICE:

PROCESS: STARTED   DONE   CANCELED   TRACKING NO.:

ORDER NO.:	NAME:		DATE:	
	CONTACT:		EMAIL:	
	ADDRESS:			

ITEM NO.	ITEM DESCRIPTION	QTY.	PRICE

NOTES:		SUBTOTAL	
		SHIPPING	
		DISCOUNT	
		TOTAL	

PAYMENT METHOD: DATE SHIPPED:

PAYMENT DATE: SHIPPING SERVICE:

PROCESS: STARTED   DONE   CANCELED   TRACKING NO.:

ORDER NO.:	NAME:		DATE:	
	CONTACT:		EMAIL:	
	ADDRESS:			

ITEM NO.	ITEM DESCRIPTION	QTY.	PRICE

NOTES:		
	SUBTOTAL	
	SHIPPING	
	DISCOUNT	
	TOTAL	

PAYMENT METHOD: DATE SHIPPED:

PAYMENT DATE: SHIPPING SERVICE:

PROCESS: STARTED DONE CANCELED   TRACKING NO.:

ORDER NO.:	NAME:		DATE:	
	CONTACT:		EMAIL:	
	ADDRESS:			

ITEM NO.	ITEM DESCRIPTION	QTY.	PRICE

NOTES:		
	SUBTOTAL	
	SHIPPING	
	DISCOUNT	
	TOTAL	

PAYMENT METHOD: DATE SHIPPED:

PAYMENT DATE: SHIPPING SERVICE:

PROCESS: STARTED DONE CANCELED   TRACKING NO.:

ORDER NO.:	NAME:		DATE:	
	CONTACT:		EMAIL:	
	ADDRESS:			

ITEM NO.	ITEM DESCRIPTION	QTY.	PRICE

NOTES:		
	SUBTOTAL	
	SHIPPING	
	DISCOUNT	
	TOTAL	

PAYMENT METHOD: DATE SHIPPED:

PAYMENT DATE: SHIPPING SERVICE:

PROCESS: STARTED   DONE   CANCELED   TRACKING NO.:

ORDER NO.:	NAME:		DATE:	
	CONTACT:		EMAIL:	
	ADDRESS:			

ITEM NO.	ITEM DESCRIPTION	QTY.	PRICE

NOTES:		
	SUBTOTAL	
	SHIPPING	
	DISCOUNT	
	TOTAL	

PAYMENT METHOD: DATE SHIPPED:

PAYMENT DATE: SHIPPING SERVICE:

PROCESS: STARTED   DONE   CANCELED   TRACKING NO.:

ORDER NO.:	NAME:		DATE:	
	CONTACT:		EMAIL:	
	ADDRESS:			

ITEM NO.	ITEM DESCRIPTION	QTY.	PRICE

NOTES:		SUBTOTAL	
		SHIPPING	
		DISCOUNT	
		TOTAL	

PAYMENT METHOD: DATE SHIPPED:

PAYMENT DATE: SHIPPING SERVICE:

PROCESS: STARTED   DONE   CANCELED   TRACKING NO.:

ORDER NO.:	NAME:		DATE:	
	CONTACT:		EMAIL:	
	ADDRESS:			

ITEM NO.	ITEM DESCRIPTION	QTY.	PRICE

NOTES:		SUBTOTAL	
		SHIPPING	
		DISCOUNT	
		TOTAL	

PAYMENT METHOD: DATE SHIPPED:

PAYMENT DATE: SHIPPING SERVICE:

PROCESS: STARTED   DONE   CANCELED   TRACKING NO.:

ORDER NO.:	NAME:		DATE:	
	CONTACT:		EMAIL:	
	ADDRESS:			

ITEM NO.	ITEM DESCRIPTION	QTY.	PRICE

NOTES:		SUBTOTAL	
		SHIPPING	
		DISCOUNT	
		TOTAL	

PAYMENT METHOD: DATE SHIPPED:

PAYMENT DATE: SHIPPING SERVICE:

PROCESS: STARTED   DONE   CANCELED   TRACKING NO.:

ORDER NO.:	NAME:		DATE:	
	CONTACT:		EMAIL:	
	ADDRESS:			

ITEM NO.	ITEM DESCRIPTION	QTY.	PRICE

NOTES:		SUBTOTAL	
		SHIPPING	
		DISCOUNT	
		TOTAL	

PAYMENT METHOD: DATE SHIPPED:

PAYMENT DATE: SHIPPING SERVICE:

PROCESS: STARTED   DONE   CANCELED   TRACKING NO.:

ORDER NO.:	NAME:		DATE:	
	CONTACT:		EMAIL:	
	ADDRESS:			

ITEM NO.	ITEM DESCRIPTION	QTY.	PRICE

NOTES:			
		SUBTOTAL	
		SHIPPING	
		DISCOUNT	
		TOTAL	

PAYMENT METHOD: DATE SHIPPED:

PAYMENT DATE: SHIPPING SERVICE:

PROCESS: STARTED   DONE   CANCELED   TRACKING NO.:

ORDER NO.:	NAME:		DATE:	
	CONTACT:		EMAIL:	
	ADDRESS:			

ITEM NO.	ITEM DESCRIPTION	QTY.	PRICE

NOTES:			
		SUBTOTAL	
		SHIPPING	
		DISCOUNT	
		TOTAL	

PAYMENT METHOD: DATE SHIPPED:

PAYMENT DATE: SHIPPING SERVICE:

PROCESS: STARTED   DONE   CANCELED   TRACKING NO.:

ORDER NO.:	NAME:		DATE:	
	CONTACT:		EMAIL:	
	ADDRESS:			

ITEM NO.	ITEM DESCRIPTION	QTY.	PRICE

NOTES:		
	SUBTOTAL	
	SHIPPING	
	DISCOUNT	
	TOTAL	

PAYMENT METHOD: DATE SHIPPED:

PAYMENT DATE: SHIPPING SERVICE:

PROCESS: STARTED   DONE   CANCELED   TRACKING NO.:

ORDER NO.:	NAME:		DATE:	
	CONTACT:		EMAIL:	
	ADDRESS:			

ITEM NO.	ITEM DESCRIPTION	QTY.	PRICE

NOTES:		
	SUBTOTAL	
	SHIPPING	
	DISCOUNT	
	TOTAL	

PAYMENT METHOD: DATE SHIPPED:

PAYMENT DATE: SHIPPING SERVICE:

PROCESS: STARTED   DONE   CANCELED   TRACKING NO.:

ORDER NO.:	NAME:		DATE:	
	CONTACT:		EMAIL:	
	ADDRESS:			

ITEM NO.	ITEM DESCRIPTION	QTY.	PRICE

NOTES:		
	SUBTOTAL	
	SHIPPING	
	DISCOUNT	
	TOTAL	

PAYMENT METHOD: DATE SHIPPED:

PAYMENT DATE: SHIPPING SERVICE:

PROCESS: STARTED   DONE   CANCELED   TRACKING NO.:

ORDER NO.:	NAME:		DATE:	
	CONTACT:		EMAIL:	
	ADDRESS:			

ITEM NO.	ITEM DESCRIPTION	QTY.	PRICE

NOTES:		
	SUBTOTAL	
	SHIPPING	
	DISCOUNT	
	TOTAL	

PAYMENT METHOD: DATE SHIPPED:

PAYMENT DATE: SHIPPING SERVICE:

PROCESS: STARTED   DONE   CANCELED   TRACKING NO.:

ORDER NO.:	NAME:		DATE:	
	CONTACT:		EMAIL:	
	ADDRESS:			

ITEM NO.	ITEM DESCRIPTION	QTY.	PRICE

NOTES:		SUBTOTAL	
		SHIPPING	
		DISCOUNT	
		TOTAL	

PAYMENT METHOD: DATE SHIPPED:

PAYMENT DATE: SHIPPING SERVICE:

PROCESS: STARTED   DONE   CANCELED   TRACKING NO.:

ORDER NO.:	NAME:		DATE:	
	CONTACT:		EMAIL:	
	ADDRESS:			

ITEM NO.	ITEM DESCRIPTION	QTY.	PRICE

NOTES:		SUBTOTAL	
		SHIPPING	
		DISCOUNT	
		TOTAL	

PAYMENT METHOD: DATE SHIPPED:

PAYMENT DATE: SHIPPING SERVICE:

PROCESS: STARTED   DONE   CANCELED   TRACKING NO.:

ORDER NO.:	NAME:			DATE:	
	CONTACT:			EMAIL:	
	ADDRESS:				

ITEM NO.	ITEM DESCRIPTION	QTY.	PRICE

NOTES:		SUBTOTAL	
		SHIPPING	
		DISCOUNT	
		TOTAL	

PAYMENT METHOD: DATE SHIPPED:

PAYMENT DATE: SHIPPING SERVICE:

PROCESS: STARTED   DONE   CANCELED   TRACKING NO.:

ORDER NO.:	NAME:			DATE:	
	CONTACT:			EMAIL:	
	ADDRESS:				

ITEM NO.	ITEM DESCRIPTION	QTY.	PRICE

NOTES:		SUBTOTAL	
		SHIPPING	
		DISCOUNT	
		TOTAL	

PAYMENT METHOD: DATE SHIPPED:

PAYMENT DATE: SHIPPING SERVICE:

PROCESS: STARTED   DONE   CANCELED   TRACKING NO.:

ORDER NO.:	NAME:		DATE:	
	CONTACT:		EMAIL:	
	ADDRESS:			

ITEM NO.	ITEM DESCRIPTION	QTY.	PRICE

NOTES:		
	SUBTOTAL	
	SHIPPING	
	DISCOUNT	
	TOTAL	

PAYMENT METHOD: DATE SHIPPED:

PAYMENT DATE: SHIPPING SERVICE:

PROCESS: STARTED   DONE   CANCELED   TRACKING NO.:

ORDER NO.:	NAME:		DATE:	
	CONTACT:		EMAIL:	
	ADDRESS:			

ITEM NO.	ITEM DESCRIPTION	QTY.	PRICE

NOTES:		
	SUBTOTAL	
	SHIPPING	
	DISCOUNT	
	TOTAL	

PAYMENT METHOD: DATE SHIPPED:

PAYMENT DATE: SHIPPING SERVICE:

PROCESS: STARTED   DONE   CANCELED   TRACKING NO.:

ORDER NO.:	NAME:		DATE:	
	CONTACT:		EMAIL:	
	ADDRESS:			

ITEM NO.	ITEM DESCRIPTION	QTY.	PRICE

NOTES:		
	SUBTOTAL	
	SHIPPING	
	DISCOUNT	
	TOTAL	

PAYMENT METHOD: DATE SHIPPED:

PAYMENT DATE: SHIPPING SERVICE:

PROCESS: STARTED   DONE   CANCELED   TRACKING NO.:

ORDER NO.:	NAME:		DATE:	
	CONTACT:		EMAIL:	
	ADDRESS:			

ITEM NO.	ITEM DESCRIPTION	QTY.	PRICE

NOTES:		
	SUBTOTAL	
	SHIPPING	
	DISCOUNT	
	TOTAL	

PAYMENT METHOD: DATE SHIPPED:

PAYMENT DATE: SHIPPING SERVICE:

PROCESS: STARTED   DONE   CANCELED   TRACKING NO.:

ORDER NO.:	NAME:		DATE:	
	CONTACT:		EMAIL:	
	ADDRESS:			

ITEM NO.	ITEM DESCRIPTION	QTY.	PRICE

NOTES:		
	SUBTOTAL	
	SHIPPING	
	DISCOUNT	
	TOTAL	

PAYMENT METHOD:　　　　　　　　　DATE SHIPPED:

PAYMENT DATE:　　　　　　　　　　SHIPPING SERVICE:

PROCESS:　STARTED　　DONE　　CANCELED　　TRACKING NO.:

ORDER NO.:	NAME:		DATE:	
	CONTACT:		EMAIL:	
	ADDRESS:			

ITEM NO.	ITEM DESCRIPTION	QTY.	PRICE

NOTES:		
	SUBTOTAL	
	SHIPPING	
	DISCOUNT	
	TOTAL	

PAYMENT METHOD:　　　　　　　　　DATE SHIPPED:

PAYMENT DATE:　　　　　　　　　　SHIPPING SERVICE:

PROCESS:　STARTED　　DONE　　CANCELED　　TRACKING NO.:

ORDER NO.:	NAME:		DATE:	
	CONTACT:		EMAIL:	
	ADDRESS:			

ITEM NO.	ITEM DESCRIPTION	QTY.	PRICE

NOTES:		SUBTOTAL	
		SHIPPING	
		DISCOUNT	
		TOTAL	

PAYMENT METHOD: DATE SHIPPED:

PAYMENT DATE: SHIPPING SERVICE:

PROCESS: STARTED   DONE   CANCELED   TRACKING NO.:

ORDER NO.:	NAME:		DATE:	
	CONTACT:		EMAIL:	
	ADDRESS:			

ITEM NO.	ITEM DESCRIPTION	QTY.	PRICE

NOTES:		SUBTOTAL	
		SHIPPING	
		DISCOUNT	
		TOTAL	

PAYMENT METHOD: DATE SHIPPED:

PAYMENT DATE: SHIPPING SERVICE:

PROCESS: STARTED   DONE   CANCELED   TRACKING NO.:

ORDER NO.:	NAME:		DATE:	
	CONTACT:		EMAIL:	
	ADDRESS:			

ITEM NO.	ITEM DESCRIPTION	QTY.	PRICE

NOTES:		
	SUBTOTAL	
	SHIPPING	
	DISCOUNT	
	TOTAL	

PAYMENT METHOD: DATE SHIPPED:

PAYMENT DATE: SHIPPING SERVICE:

PROCESS: STARTED   DONE   CANCELED   TRACKING NO.:

ORDER NO.:	NAME:		DATE:	
	CONTACT:		EMAIL:	
	ADDRESS:			

ITEM NO.	ITEM DESCRIPTION	QTY.	PRICE

NOTES:		
	SUBTOTAL	
	SHIPPING	
	DISCOUNT	
	TOTAL	

PAYMENT METHOD: DATE SHIPPED:

PAYMENT DATE: SHIPPING SERVICE:

PROCESS: STARTED   DONE   CANCELED   TRACKING NO.:

ORDER NO.:	NAME:		DATE:	
	CONTACT:		EMAIL:	
	ADDRESS:			

ITEM NO.	ITEM DESCRIPTION	QTY.	PRICE

NOTES:		
	SUBTOTAL	
	SHIPPING	
	DISCOUNT	
	TOTAL	

PAYMENT METHOD: DATE SHIPPED:

PAYMENT DATE: SHIPPING SERVICE:

PROCESS: STARTED   DONE   CANCELED   TRACKING NO.:

ORDER NO.:	NAME:		DATE:	
	CONTACT:		EMAIL:	
	ADDRESS:			

ITEM NO.	ITEM DESCRIPTION	QTY.	PRICE

NOTES:		
	SUBTOTAL	
	SHIPPING	
	DISCOUNT	
	TOTAL	

PAYMENT METHOD: DATE SHIPPED:

PAYMENT DATE: SHIPPING SERVICE:

PROCESS: STARTED   DONE   CANCELED   TRACKING NO.:

ORDER NO.:	NAME:		DATE:	
	CONTACT:		EMAIL:	
	ADDRESS:			

ITEM NO.	ITEM DESCRIPTION	QTY.	PRICE

NOTES:		
	SUBTOTAL	
	SHIPPING	
	DISCOUNT	
	TOTAL	

PAYMENT METHOD: DATE SHIPPED:

PAYMENT DATE: SHIPPING SERVICE:

PROCESS: STARTED   DONE   CANCELED   TRACKING NO.:

ORDER NO.:	NAME:		DATE:	
	CONTACT:		EMAIL:	
	ADDRESS:			

ITEM NO.	ITEM DESCRIPTION	QTY.	PRICE

NOTES:		
	SUBTOTAL	
	SHIPPING	
	DISCOUNT	
	TOTAL	

PAYMENT METHOD: DATE SHIPPED:

PAYMENT DATE: SHIPPING SERVICE:

PROCESS: STARTED   DONE   CANCELED   TRACKING NO.:

ORDER NO.:	NAME:				DATE:		
	CONTACT:				EMAIL:		
	ADDRESS:						

ITEM NO.	ITEM DESCRIPTION	QTY.	PRICE

NOTES:		
	SUBTOTAL	
	SHIPPING	
	DISCOUNT	
	TOTAL	

PAYMENT METHOD: DATE SHIPPED:

PAYMENT DATE: SHIPPING SERVICE:

PROCESS: STARTED   DONE   CANCELED   TRACKING NO.:

ORDER NO.:	NAME:				DATE:		
	CONTACT:				EMAIL:		
	ADDRESS:						

ITEM NO.	ITEM DESCRIPTION	QTY.	PRICE

NOTES:		
	SUBTOTAL	
	SHIPPING	
	DISCOUNT	
	TOTAL	

PAYMENT METHOD: DATE SHIPPED:

PAYMENT DATE: SHIPPING SERVICE:

PROCESS: STARTED   DONE   CANCELED   TRACKING NO.:

ORDER NO.:	NAME:		DATE:	
	CONTACT:		EMAIL:	
	ADDRESS:			

ITEM NO.	ITEM DESCRIPTION	QTY.	PRICE

NOTES:		
	SUBTOTAL	
	SHIPPING	
	DISCOUNT	
	TOTAL	

PAYMENT METHOD: DATE SHIPPED:

PAYMENT DATE: SHIPPING SERVICE:

PROCESS: STARTED   DONE   CANCELED   TRACKING NO.:

ORDER NO.:	NAME:		DATE:	
	CONTACT:		EMAIL:	
	ADDRESS:			

ITEM NO.	ITEM DESCRIPTION	QTY.	PRICE

NOTES:		
	SUBTOTAL	
	SHIPPING	
	DISCOUNT	
	TOTAL	

PAYMENT METHOD: DATE SHIPPED:

PAYMENT DATE: SHIPPING SERVICE:

PROCESS: STARTED   DONE   CANCELED   TRACKING NO.:

ORDER NO.:	NAME:		DATE:	
	CONTACT:		EMAIL:	
	ADDRESS:			

ITEM NO.	ITEM DESCRIPTION	QTY.	PRICE

NOTES:		
	SUBTOTAL	
	SHIPPING	
	DISCOUNT	
	TOTAL	

PAYMENT METHOD: DATE SHIPPED:

PAYMENT DATE: SHIPPING SERVICE:

PROCESS: STARTED   DONE   CANCELED   TRACKING NO.:

ORDER NO.:	NAME:		DATE:	
	CONTACT:		EMAIL:	
	ADDRESS:			

ITEM NO.	ITEM DESCRIPTION	QTY.	PRICE

NOTES:		
	SUBTOTAL	
	SHIPPING	
	DISCOUNT	
	TOTAL	

PAYMENT METHOD: DATE SHIPPED:

PAYMENT DATE: SHIPPING SERVICE:

PROCESS: STARTED   DONE   CANCELED   TRACKING NO.:

ORDER NO.:	NAME:		DATE:	
	CONTACT:		EMAIL:	
	ADDRESS:			

ITEM NO.	ITEM DESCRIPTION	QTY.	PRICE

NOTES:			
	SUBTOTAL	
	SHIPPING	
	DISCOUNT	
	TOTAL	

PAYMENT METHOD: DATE SHIPPED:

PAYMENT DATE: SHIPPING SERVICE:

PROCESS: STARTED DONE CANCELED TRACKING NO.:

ORDER NO.:	NAME:		DATE:	
	CONTACT:		EMAIL:	
	ADDRESS:			

ITEM NO.	ITEM DESCRIPTION	QTY.	PRICE

NOTES:			
	SUBTOTAL	
	SHIPPING	
	DISCOUNT	
	TOTAL	

PAYMENT METHOD: DATE SHIPPED:

PAYMENT DATE: SHIPPING SERVICE:

PROCESS: STARTED DONE CANCELED TRACKING NO.:

ORDER NO.:	NAME:		DATE:	
	CONTACT:		EMAIL:	
	ADDRESS:			

ITEM NO.	ITEM DESCRIPTION	QTY.	PRICE

NOTES:		SUBTOTAL	
		SHIPPING	
		DISCOUNT	
		TOTAL	

PAYMENT METHOD: DATE SHIPPED:

PAYMENT DATE: SHIPPING SERVICE:

PROCESS: STARTED   DONE   CANCELED   TRACKING NO.:

ORDER NO.:	NAME:		DATE:	
	CONTACT:		EMAIL:	
	ADDRESS:			

ITEM NO.	ITEM DESCRIPTION	QTY.	PRICE

NOTES:		SUBTOTAL	
		SHIPPING	
		DISCOUNT	
		TOTAL	

PAYMENT METHOD: DATE SHIPPED:

PAYMENT DATE: SHIPPING SERVICE:

PROCESS: STARTED   DONE   CANCELED   TRACKING NO.:

ORDER NO.:	NAME:		DATE:	
	CONTACT:		EMAIL:	
	ADDRESS:			

ITEM NO.	ITEM DESCRIPTION	QTY.	PRICE

NOTES:	SUBTOTAL	
	SHIPPING	
	DISCOUNT	
	TOTAL	

PAYMENT METHOD: DATE SHIPPED:

PAYMENT DATE: SHIPPING SERVICE:

PROCESS: STARTED   DONE   CANCELED   TRACKING NO.:

ORDER NO.:	NAME:		DATE:	
	CONTACT:		EMAIL:	
	ADDRESS:			

ITEM NO.	ITEM DESCRIPTION	QTY.	PRICE

NOTES:	SUBTOTAL	
	SHIPPING	
	DISCOUNT	
	TOTAL	

PAYMENT METHOD: DATE SHIPPED:

PAYMENT DATE: SHIPPING SERVICE:

PROCESS: STARTED   DONE   CANCELED   TRACKING NO.:

ORDER NO.:	NAME:		DATE:	
	CONTACT:		EMAIL:	
	ADDRESS:			

ITEM NO.	ITEM DESCRIPTION	QTY.	PRICE

NOTES:		SUBTOTAL	
		SHIPPING	
		DISCOUNT	
		TOTAL	

PAYMENT METHOD: DATE SHIPPED:

PAYMENT DATE: SHIPPING SERVICE:

PROCESS: STARTED   DONE   CANCELED   TRACKING NO.:

ORDER NO.:	NAME:		DATE:	
	CONTACT:		EMAIL:	
	ADDRESS:			

ITEM NO.	ITEM DESCRIPTION	QTY.	PRICE

NOTES:		SUBTOTAL	
		SHIPPING	
		DISCOUNT	
		TOTAL	

PAYMENT METHOD: DATE SHIPPED:

PAYMENT DATE: SHIPPING SERVICE:

PROCESS: STARTED   DONE   CANCELED   TRACKING NO.:

ORDER NO.:	NAME:		DATE:	
	CONTACT:		EMAIL:	
	ADDRESS:			

ITEM NO.	ITEM DESCRIPTION	QTY.	PRICE

NOTES:	SUBTOTAL	
	SHIPPING	
	DISCOUNT	
	TOTAL	

PAYMENT METHOD: DATE SHIPPED:

PAYMENT DATE: SHIPPING SERVICE:

PROCESS: STARTED   DONE   CANCELED   TRACKING NO.:

ORDER NO.:	NAME:		DATE:	
	CONTACT:		EMAIL:	
	ADDRESS:			

ITEM NO.	ITEM DESCRIPTION	QTY.	PRICE

NOTES:	SUBTOTAL	
	SHIPPING	
	DISCOUNT	
	TOTAL	

PAYMENT METHOD: DATE SHIPPED:

PAYMENT DATE: SHIPPING SERVICE:

PROCESS: STARTED   DONE   CANCELED   TRACKING NO.:

ORDER NO.:	NAME:		DATE:	
	CONTACT:		EMAIL:	
	ADDRESS:			

ITEM NO.	ITEM DESCRIPTION	QTY.	PRICE

NOTES:		SUBTOTAL	
		SHIPPING	
		DISCOUNT	
		TOTAL	

PAYMENT METHOD: DATE SHIPPED:

PAYMENT DATE: SHIPPING SERVICE:

PROCESS: STARTED   DONE   CANCELED   TRACKING NO.:

ORDER NO.:	NAME:		DATE:	
	CONTACT:		EMAIL:	
	ADDRESS:			

ITEM NO.	ITEM DESCRIPTION	QTY.	PRICE

NOTES:		SUBTOTAL	
		SHIPPING	
		DISCOUNT	
		TOTAL	

PAYMENT METHOD: DATE SHIPPED:

PAYMENT DATE: SHIPPING SERVICE:

PROCESS: STARTED   DONE   CANCELED   TRACKING NO.:

ORDER NO.:	NAME:			DATE:	
	CONTACT:			EMAIL:	
	ADDRESS:				

ITEM NO.	ITEM DESCRIPTION	QTY.	PRICE

NOTES:		
	SUBTOTAL	
	SHIPPING	
	DISCOUNT	
	TOTAL	

PAYMENT METHOD: DATE SHIPPED:

PAYMENT DATE: SHIPPING SERVICE:

PROCESS: STARTED DONE CANCELED TRACKING NO.:

ORDER NO.:	NAME:			DATE:	
	CONTACT:			EMAIL:	
	ADDRESS:				

ITEM NO.	ITEM DESCRIPTION	QTY.	PRICE

NOTES:		
	SUBTOTAL	
	SHIPPING	
	DISCOUNT	
	TOTAL	

PAYMENT METHOD: DATE SHIPPED:

PAYMENT DATE: SHIPPING SERVICE:

PROCESS: STARTED DONE CANCELED TRACKING NO.:

ORDER NO.:	NAME:		DATE:	
	CONTACT:		EMAIL:	
	ADDRESS:			

ITEM NO.	ITEM DESCRIPTION	QTY.	PRICE

NOTES:		SUBTOTAL	
		SHIPPING	
		DISCOUNT	
		TOTAL	

PAYMENT METHOD: DATE SHIPPED:

PAYMENT DATE: SHIPPING SERVICE:

PROCESS: STARTED   DONE   CANCELED   TRACKING NO.:

ORDER NO.:	NAME:		DATE:	
	CONTACT:		EMAIL:	
	ADDRESS:			

ITEM NO.	ITEM DESCRIPTION	QTY.	PRICE

NOTES:		SUBTOTAL	
		SHIPPING	
		DISCOUNT	
		TOTAL	

PAYMENT METHOD: DATE SHIPPED:

PAYMENT DATE: SHIPPING SERVICE:

PROCESS: STARTED   DONE   CANCELED   TRACKING NO.:

ORDER NO.:	NAME:		DATE:	
	CONTACT:		EMAIL:	
	ADDRESS:			

ITEM NO.	ITEM DESCRIPTION	QTY.	PRICE

NOTES:	SUBTOTAL	
	SHIPPING	
	DISCOUNT	
	TOTAL	

PAYMENT METHOD: DATE SHIPPED:

PAYMENT DATE: SHIPPING SERVICE:

PROCESS: STARTED   DONE   CANCELED   TRACKING NO.:

ORDER NO.:	NAME:		DATE:	
	CONTACT:		EMAIL:	
	ADDRESS:			

ITEM NO.	ITEM DESCRIPTION	QTY.	PRICE

NOTES:	SUBTOTAL	
	SHIPPING	
	DISCOUNT	
	TOTAL	

PAYMENT METHOD: DATE SHIPPED:

PAYMENT DATE: SHIPPING SERVICE:

PROCESS: STARTED   DONE   CANCELED   TRACKING NO.:

ORDER NO.:	NAME:		DATE:	
	CONTACT:		EMAIL:	
	ADDRESS:			

ITEM NO.	ITEM DESCRIPTION	QTY.	PRICE

NOTES:		SUBTOTAL	
		SHIPPING	
		DISCOUNT	
		TOTAL	

PAYMENT METHOD: DATE SHIPPED:

PAYMENT DATE: SHIPPING SERVICE:

PROCESS: STARTED   DONE   CANCELED   TRACKING NO.:

ORDER NO.:	NAME:		DATE:	
	CONTACT:		EMAIL:	
	ADDRESS:			

ITEM NO.	ITEM DESCRIPTION	QTY.	PRICE

NOTES:		SUBTOTAL	
		SHIPPING	
		DISCOUNT	
		TOTAL	

PAYMENT METHOD: DATE SHIPPED:

PAYMENT DATE: SHIPPING SERVICE:

PROCESS: STARTED   DONE   CANCELED   TRACKING NO.:

ORDER NO.:	NAME:		DATE:	
	CONTACT:		EMAIL:	
	ADDRESS:			

ITEM NO.	ITEM DESCRIPTION	QTY.	PRICE

NOTES:		
	SUBTOTAL	
	SHIPPING	
	DISCOUNT	
	TOTAL	

PAYMENT METHOD: DATE SHIPPED:

PAYMENT DATE: SHIPPING SERVICE:

PROCESS: STARTED   DONE   CANCELED   TRACKING NO.:

ORDER NO.:	NAME:		DATE:	
	CONTACT:		EMAIL:	
	ADDRESS:			

ITEM NO.	ITEM DESCRIPTION	QTY.	PRICE

NOTES:		
	SUBTOTAL	
	SHIPPING	
	DISCOUNT	
	TOTAL	

PAYMENT METHOD: DATE SHIPPED:

PAYMENT DATE: SHIPPING SERVICE:

PROCESS: STARTED   DONE   CANCELED   TRACKING NO.:

ORDER NO.:	NAME:		DATE:	
	CONTACT:		EMAIL:	
	ADDRESS:			

ITEM NO.	ITEM DESCRIPTION	QTY.	PRICE

NOTES:		SUBTOTAL	
		SHIPPING	
		DISCOUNT	
		TOTAL	

PAYMENT METHOD: DATE SHIPPED:

PAYMENT DATE: SHIPPING SERVICE:

PROCESS: STARTED DONE CANCELED TRACKING NO.:

ORDER NO.:	NAME:		DATE:	
	CONTACT:		EMAIL:	
	ADDRESS:			

ITEM NO.	ITEM DESCRIPTION	QTY.	PRICE

NOTES:		SUBTOTAL	
		SHIPPING	
		DISCOUNT	
		TOTAL	

PAYMENT METHOD: DATE SHIPPED:

PAYMENT DATE: SHIPPING SERVICE:

PROCESS: STARTED DONE CANCELED TRACKING NO.:

ORDER NO.:	NAME:		DATE:	
	CONTACT:		EMAIL:	
	ADDRESS:			

ITEM NO.	ITEM DESCRIPTION	QTY.	PRICE

NOTES:		
	SUBTOTAL	
	SHIPPING	
	DISCOUNT	
	TOTAL	

PAYMENT METHOD: DATE SHIPPED:

PAYMENT DATE: SHIPPING SERVICE:

PROCESS: STARTED   DONE   CANCELED   TRACKING NO.:

ORDER NO.:	NAME:		DATE:	
	CONTACT:		EMAIL:	
	ADDRESS:			

ITEM NO.	ITEM DESCRIPTION	QTY.	PRICE

NOTES:		
	SUBTOTAL	
	SHIPPING	
	DISCOUNT	
	TOTAL	

PAYMENT METHOD: DATE SHIPPED:

PAYMENT DATE: SHIPPING SERVICE:

PROCESS: STARTED   DONE   CANCELED   TRACKING NO.:

ORDER NO.:	NAME:		DATE:	
	CONTACT:		EMAIL:	
	ADDRESS:			

ITEM NO.	ITEM DESCRIPTION	QTY.	PRICE

NOTES:		SUBTOTAL	
		SHIPPING	
		DISCOUNT	
		TOTAL	

PAYMENT METHOD: DATE SHIPPED:

PAYMENT DATE: SHIPPING SERVICE:

PROCESS: STARTED   DONE   CANCELED   TRACKING NO.:

ORDER NO.:	NAME:		DATE:	
	CONTACT:		EMAIL:	
	ADDRESS:			

ITEM NO.	ITEM DESCRIPTION	QTY.	PRICE

NOTES:		SUBTOTAL	
		SHIPPING	
		DISCOUNT	
		TOTAL	

PAYMENT METHOD: DATE SHIPPED:

PAYMENT DATE: SHIPPING SERVICE:

PROCESS: STARTED   DONE   CANCELED   TRACKING NO.:

ORDER NO.:	NAME:		DATE:	
	CONTACT:		EMAIL:	
	ADDRESS:			

ITEM NO.	ITEM DESCRIPTION	QTY.	PRICE

NOTES:		
	SUBTOTAL	
	SHIPPING	
	DISCOUNT	
	TOTAL	

PAYMENT METHOD: DATE SHIPPED:

PAYMENT DATE: SHIPPING SERVICE:

PROCESS: STARTED   DONE   CANCELED   TRACKING NO.:

ORDER NO.:	NAME:		DATE:	
	CONTACT:		EMAIL:	
	ADDRESS:			

ITEM NO.	ITEM DESCRIPTION	QTY.	PRICE

NOTES:		
	SUBTOTAL	
	SHIPPING	
	DISCOUNT	
	TOTAL	

PAYMENT METHOD: DATE SHIPPED:

PAYMENT DATE: SHIPPING SERVICE:

PROCESS: STARTED   DONE   CANCELED   TRACKING NO.:

ORDER NO.:	NAME:		DATE:	
	CONTACT:		EMAIL:	
	ADDRESS:			

ITEM NO.	ITEM DESCRIPTION	QTY.	PRICE

NOTES:	SUBTOTAL	
	SHIPPING	
	DISCOUNT	
	TOTAL	

PAYMENT METHOD: DATE SHIPPED:

PAYMENT DATE: SHIPPING SERVICE:

PROCESS: STARTED   DONE   CANCELED   TRACKING NO.:

ORDER NO.:	NAME:		DATE:	
	CONTACT:		EMAIL:	
	ADDRESS:			

ITEM NO.	ITEM DESCRIPTION	QTY.	PRICE

NOTES:	SUBTOTAL	
	SHIPPING	
	DISCOUNT	
	TOTAL	

PAYMENT METHOD: DATE SHIPPED:

PAYMENT DATE: SHIPPING SERVICE:

PROCESS: STARTED   DONE   CANCELED   TRACKING NO.:

ORDER NO.:	NAME:		DATE:	
	CONTACT:		EMAIL:	
	ADDRESS:			

ITEM NO.	ITEM DESCRIPTION	QTY.	PRICE

NOTES:	SUBTOTAL	
	SHIPPING	
	DISCOUNT	
	TOTAL	

PAYMENT METHOD: DATE SHIPPED:

PAYMENT DATE: SHIPPING SERVICE:

PROCESS: STARTED   DONE   CANCELED   TRACKING NO.:

ORDER NO.:	NAME:		DATE:	
	CONTACT:		EMAIL:	
	ADDRESS:			

ITEM NO.	ITEM DESCRIPTION	QTY.	PRICE

NOTES:	SUBTOTAL	
	SHIPPING	
	DISCOUNT	
	TOTAL	

PAYMENT METHOD: DATE SHIPPED:

PAYMENT DATE: SHIPPING SERVICE:

PROCESS: STARTED   DONE   CANCELED   TRACKING NO.:

ORDER NO.:	NAME:		DATE:	
	CONTACT:		EMAIL:	
	ADDRESS:			

ITEM NO.	ITEM DESCRIPTION	QTY.	PRICE

NOTES:		
	SUBTOTAL	
	SHIPPING	
	DISCOUNT	
	TOTAL	

PAYMENT METHOD: DATE SHIPPED:

PAYMENT DATE: SHIPPING SERVICE:

PROCESS: STARTED   DONE   CANCELED   TRACKING NO.:

ORDER NO.:	NAME:		DATE:	
	CONTACT:		EMAIL:	
	ADDRESS:			

ITEM NO.	ITEM DESCRIPTION	QTY.	PRICE

NOTES:		
	SUBTOTAL	
	SHIPPING	
	DISCOUNT	
	TOTAL	

PAYMENT METHOD: DATE SHIPPED:

PAYMENT DATE: SHIPPING SERVICE:

PROCESS: STARTED   DONE   CANCELED   TRACKING NO.:

ORDER NO.:	NAME:		DATE:	
	CONTACT:		EMAIL:	
	ADDRESS:			

ITEM NO.	ITEM DESCRIPTION	QTY.	PRICE

NOTES:		SUBTOTAL	
		SHIPPING	
		DISCOUNT	
		TOTAL	

PAYMENT METHOD: DATE SHIPPED:

PAYMENT DATE: SHIPPING SERVICE:

PROCESS: STARTED   DONE   CANCELED   TRACKING NO.:

ORDER NO.:	NAME:		DATE:	
	CONTACT:		EMAIL:	
	ADDRESS:			

ITEM NO.	ITEM DESCRIPTION	QTY.	PRICE

NOTES:		SUBTOTAL	
		SHIPPING	
		DISCOUNT	
		TOTAL	

PAYMENT METHOD: DATE SHIPPED:

PAYMENT DATE: SHIPPING SERVICE:

PROCESS: STARTED   DONE   CANCELED   TRACKING NO.:

ORDER NO.:	NAME:		DATE:	
	CONTACT:		EMAIL:	
	ADDRESS:			

ITEM NO.	ITEM DESCRIPTION	QTY.	PRICE

NOTES:		
	SUBTOTAL	
	SHIPPING	
	DISCOUNT	
	TOTAL	

PAYMENT METHOD: DATE SHIPPED:

PAYMENT DATE: SHIPPING SERVICE:

PROCESS: STARTED   DONE   CANCELED   TRACKING NO.:

ORDER NO.:	NAME:		DATE:	
	CONTACT:		EMAIL:	
	ADDRESS:			

ITEM NO.	ITEM DESCRIPTION	QTY.	PRICE

NOTES:		
	SUBTOTAL	
	SHIPPING	
	DISCOUNT	
	TOTAL	

PAYMENT METHOD: DATE SHIPPED:

PAYMENT DATE: SHIPPING SERVICE:

PROCESS: STARTED   DONE   CANCELED   TRACKING NO.:

ORDER NO.:	NAME:		DATE:	
	CONTACT:		EMAIL:	
	ADDRESS:			

ITEM NO.	ITEM DESCRIPTION	QTY.	PRICE

NOTES:		
	SUBTOTAL	
	SHIPPING	
	DISCOUNT	
	TOTAL	

PAYMENT METHOD: DATE SHIPPED:

PAYMENT DATE: SHIPPING SERVICE:

PROCESS: STARTED   DONE   CANCELED   TRACKING NO.:

ORDER NO.:	NAME:		DATE:	
	CONTACT:		EMAIL:	
	ADDRESS:			

ITEM NO.	ITEM DESCRIPTION	QTY.	PRICE

NOTES:		
	SUBTOTAL	
	SHIPPING	
	DISCOUNT	
	TOTAL	

PAYMENT METHOD: DATE SHIPPED:

PAYMENT DATE: SHIPPING SERVICE:

PROCESS: STARTED   DONE   CANCELED   TRACKING NO.:

ORDER NO.:	NAME:		DATE:	
	CONTACT:		EMAIL:	
	ADDRESS:			

ITEM NO.	ITEM DESCRIPTION	QTY.	PRICE

NOTES:		
	SUBTOTAL	
	SHIPPING	
	DISCOUNT	
	TOTAL	

PAYMENT METHOD: DATE SHIPPED:

PAYMENT DATE: SHIPPING SERVICE:

PROCESS: STARTED   DONE   CANCELED   TRACKING NO.:

ORDER NO.:	NAME:		DATE:	
	CONTACT:		EMAIL:	
	ADDRESS:			

ITEM NO.	ITEM DESCRIPTION	QTY.	PRICE

NOTES:		
	SUBTOTAL	
	SHIPPING	
	DISCOUNT	
	TOTAL	

PAYMENT METHOD: DATE SHIPPED:

PAYMENT DATE: SHIPPING SERVICE:

PROCESS: STARTED   DONE   CANCELED   TRACKING NO.:

ORDER NO.:	NAME:		DATE:	
	CONTACT:		EMAIL:	
	ADDRESS:			

ITEM NO.	ITEM DESCRIPTION	QTY.	PRICE

NOTES:		
	SUBTOTAL	
	SHIPPING	
	DISCOUNT	
	TOTAL	

PAYMENT METHOD: DATE SHIPPED:

PAYMENT DATE: SHIPPING SERVICE:

PROCESS: STARTED   DONE   CANCELED   TRACKING NO.:

ORDER NO.:	NAME:		DATE:	
	CONTACT:		EMAIL:	
	ADDRESS:			

ITEM NO.	ITEM DESCRIPTION	QTY.	PRICE

NOTES:		
	SUBTOTAL	
	SHIPPING	
	DISCOUNT	
	TOTAL	

PAYMENT METHOD: DATE SHIPPED:

PAYMENT DATE: SHIPPING SERVICE:

PROCESS: STARTED   DONE   CANCELED   TRACKING NO.:

ORDER NO.:	NAME:		DATE:	
	CONTACT:		EMAIL:	
	ADDRESS:			

ITEM NO.	ITEM DESCRIPTION	QTY.	PRICE

NOTES:		
	SUBTOTAL	
	SHIPPING	
	DISCOUNT	
	TOTAL	

PAYMENT METHOD: DATE SHIPPED:

PAYMENT DATE: SHIPPING SERVICE:

PROCESS: STARTED   DONE   CANCELED   TRACKING NO.:

ORDER NO.:	NAME:		DATE:	
	CONTACT:		EMAIL:	
	ADDRESS:			

ITEM NO.	ITEM DESCRIPTION	QTY.	PRICE

NOTES:		
	SUBTOTAL	
	SHIPPING	
	DISCOUNT	
	TOTAL	

PAYMENT METHOD: DATE SHIPPED:

PAYMENT DATE: SHIPPING SERVICE:

PROCESS: STARTED   DONE   CANCELED   TRACKING NO.:

ORDER NO.:	NAME:		DATE:	
	CONTACT:		EMAIL:	
	ADDRESS:			

ITEM NO.	ITEM DESCRIPTION	QTY.	PRICE

NOTES:			
	SUBTOTAL		
	SHIPPING		
	DISCOUNT		
	TOTAL		

PAYMENT METHOD: DATE SHIPPED:

PAYMENT DATE: SHIPPING SERVICE:

PROCESS: STARTED   DONE   CANCELED   TRACKING NO.:

ORDER NO.:	NAME:		DATE:	
	CONTACT:		EMAIL:	
	ADDRESS:			

ITEM NO.	ITEM DESCRIPTION	QTY.	PRICE

NOTES:			
	SUBTOTAL		
	SHIPPING		
	DISCOUNT		
	TOTAL		

PAYMENT METHOD: DATE SHIPPED:

PAYMENT DATE: SHIPPING SERVICE:

PROCESS: STARTED   DONE   CANCELED   TRACKING NO.:

ORDER NO.:	NAME:		DATE:	
	CONTACT:		EMAIL:	
	ADDRESS:			

ITEM NO.	ITEM DESCRIPTION	QTY.	PRICE

NOTES:		
	SUBTOTAL	
	SHIPPING	
	DISCOUNT	
	TOTAL	

PAYMENT METHOD: DATE SHIPPED:

PAYMENT DATE: SHIPPING SERVICE:

PROCESS: STARTED DONE CANCELED TRACKING NO.:

ORDER NO.:	NAME:		DATE:	
	CONTACT:		EMAIL:	
	ADDRESS:			

ITEM NO.	ITEM DESCRIPTION	QTY.	PRICE

NOTES:		
	SUBTOTAL	
	SHIPPING	
	DISCOUNT	
	TOTAL	

PAYMENT METHOD: DATE SHIPPED:

PAYMENT DATE: SHIPPING SERVICE:

PROCESS: STARTED DONE CANCELED TRACKING NO.:

ORDER NO.:	NAME:		DATE:	
	CONTACT:		EMAIL:	
	ADDRESS:			

ITEM NO.	ITEM DESCRIPTION	QTY.	PRICE

NOTES:		
	SUBTOTAL	
	SHIPPING	
	DISCOUNT	
	TOTAL	

PAYMENT METHOD: DATE SHIPPED:

PAYMENT DATE: SHIPPING SERVICE:

PROCESS: STARTED   DONE   CANCELED   TRACKING NO.:

ORDER NO.:	NAME:		DATE:	
	CONTACT:		EMAIL:	
	ADDRESS:			

ITEM NO.	ITEM DESCRIPTION	QTY.	PRICE

NOTES:		
	SUBTOTAL	
	SHIPPING	
	DISCOUNT	
	TOTAL	

PAYMENT METHOD: DATE SHIPPED:

PAYMENT DATE: SHIPPING SERVICE:

PROCESS: STARTED   DONE   CANCELED   TRACKING NO.:

ORDER NO.:	NAME:		DATE:	
	CONTACT:		EMAIL:	
	ADDRESS:			

ITEM NO.	ITEM DESCRIPTION	QTY.	PRICE

NOTES:		
	SUBTOTAL	
	SHIPPING	
	DISCOUNT	
	TOTAL	

PAYMENT METHOD: DATE SHIPPED:

PAYMENT DATE: SHIPPING SERVICE:

PROCESS: STARTED DONE CANCELED TRACKING NO.:

ORDER NO.:	NAME:		DATE:	
	CONTACT:		EMAIL:	
	ADDRESS:			

ITEM NO.	ITEM DESCRIPTION	QTY.	PRICE

NOTES:		
	SUBTOTAL	
	SHIPPING	
	DISCOUNT	
	TOTAL	

PAYMENT METHOD: DATE SHIPPED:

PAYMENT DATE: SHIPPING SERVICE:

PROCESS: STARTED DONE CANCELED TRACKING NO.:

ORDER NO.:	NAME:		DATE:	
	CONTACT:		EMAIL:	
	ADDRESS:			

ITEM NO.	ITEM DESCRIPTION	QTY.	PRICE

NOTES:		
	SUBTOTAL	
	SHIPPING	
	DISCOUNT	
	TOTAL	

PAYMENT METHOD: DATE SHIPPED:

PAYMENT DATE: SHIPPING SERVICE:

PROCESS: STARTED   DONE   CANCELED   TRACKING NO.:

ORDER NO.:	NAME:		DATE:	
	CONTACT:		EMAIL:	
	ADDRESS:			

ITEM NO.	ITEM DESCRIPTION	QTY.	PRICE

NOTES:		
	SUBTOTAL	
	SHIPPING	
	DISCOUNT	
	TOTAL	

PAYMENT METHOD: DATE SHIPPED:

PAYMENT DATE: SHIPPING SERVICE:

PROCESS: STARTED   DONE   CANCELED   TRACKING NO.:

ORDER NO.:	NAME:		DATE:	
	CONTACT:		EMAIL:	
	ADDRESS:			

ITEM NO.	ITEM DESCRIPTION	QTY.	PRICE

NOTES:		
	SUBTOTAL	
	SHIPPING	
	DISCOUNT	
	TOTAL	

PAYMENT METHOD: DATE SHIPPED:

PAYMENT DATE: SHIPPING SERVICE:

PROCESS: STARTED   DONE   CANCELED   TRACKING NO.:

ORDER NO.:	NAME:		DATE:	
	CONTACT:		EMAIL:	
	ADDRESS:			

ITEM NO.	ITEM DESCRIPTION	QTY.	PRICE

NOTES:		
	SUBTOTAL	
	SHIPPING	
	DISCOUNT	
	TOTAL	

PAYMENT METHOD: DATE SHIPPED:

PAYMENT DATE: SHIPPING SERVICE:

PROCESS: STARTED   DONE   CANCELED   TRACKING NO.:

ORDER NO.:

NAME:		DATE:
CONTACT:		EMAIL:
ADDRESS:		

ITEM NO.	ITEM DESCRIPTION	QTY.	PRICE

NOTES:		
	SUBTOTAL	
	SHIPPING	
	DISCOUNT	
	TOTAL	

PAYMENT METHOD: DATE SHIPPED:

PAYMENT DATE: SHIPPING SERVICE:

PROCESS: STARTED   DONE   CANCELED   TRACKING NO.:

ORDER NO.:

NAME:		DATE:
CONTACT:		EMAIL:
ADDRESS:		

ITEM NO.	ITEM DESCRIPTION	QTY.	PRICE

NOTES:		
	SUBTOTAL	
	SHIPPING	
	DISCOUNT	
	TOTAL	

PAYMENT METHOD: DATE SHIPPED:

PAYMENT DATE: SHIPPING SERVICE:

PROCESS: STARTED   DONE   CANCELED   TRACKING NO.:

ORDER NO.:

NAME:		DATE:
CONTACT:		EMAIL:
ADDRESS:		

ITEM NO.	ITEM DESCRIPTION	QTY.	PRICE

NOTES:		SUBTOTAL	
		SHIPPING	
		DISCOUNT	
		TOTAL	

PAYMENT METHOD: DATE SHIPPED:

PAYMENT DATE: SHIPPING SERVICE:

PROCESS: STARTED   DONE   CANCELED   TRACKING NO.:

ORDER NO.:

NAME:		DATE:
CONTACT:		EMAIL:
ADDRESS:		

ITEM NO.	ITEM DESCRIPTION	QTY.	PRICE

NOTES:		SUBTOTAL	
		SHIPPING	
		DISCOUNT	
		TOTAL	

PAYMENT METHOD: DATE SHIPPED:

PAYMENT DATE: SHIPPING SERVICE:

PROCESS: STARTED   DONE   CANCELED   TRACKING NO.:

ORDER NO.:	NAME:		DATE:	
	CONTACT:		EMAIL:	
	ADDRESS:			

ITEM NO.	ITEM DESCRIPTION	QTY.	PRICE

NOTES:		
	SUBTOTAL	
	SHIPPING	
	DISCOUNT	
	TOTAL	

PAYMENT METHOD: DATE SHIPPED:

PAYMENT DATE: SHIPPING SERVICE:

PROCESS: STARTED   DONE   CANCELED   TRACKING NO.:

ORDER NO.:	NAME:		DATE:	
	CONTACT:		EMAIL:	
	ADDRESS:			

ITEM NO.	ITEM DESCRIPTION	QTY.	PRICE

NOTES:		
	SUBTOTAL	
	SHIPPING	
	DISCOUNT	
	TOTAL	

PAYMENT METHOD: DATE SHIPPED:

PAYMENT DATE: SHIPPING SERVICE:

PROCESS: STARTED   DONE   CANCELED   TRACKING NO.:

ORDER NO.:	NAME:		DATE:	
	CONTACT:		EMAIL:	
	ADDRESS:			

ITEM NO.	ITEM DESCRIPTION	QTY.	PRICE

NOTES:		SUBTOTAL	
		SHIPPING	
		DISCOUNT	
		TOTAL	

PAYMENT METHOD: DATE SHIPPED:

PAYMENT DATE: SHIPPING SERVICE:

PROCESS: STARTED   DONE   CANCELED   TRACKING NO.:

ORDER NO.:	NAME:		DATE:	
	CONTACT:		EMAIL:	
	ADDRESS:			

ITEM NO.	ITEM DESCRIPTION	QTY.	PRICE

NOTES:		SUBTOTAL	
		SHIPPING	
		DISCOUNT	
		TOTAL	

PAYMENT METHOD: DATE SHIPPED:

PAYMENT DATE: SHIPPING SERVICE:

PROCESS: STARTED   DONE   CANCELED   TRACKING NO.:

ORDER NO.:	NAME:		DATE:	
	CONTACT:		EMAIL:	
	ADDRESS:			

ITEM NO.	ITEM DESCRIPTION	QTY.	PRICE

NOTES:		SUBTOTAL	
		SHIPPING	
		DISCOUNT	
		TOTAL	

PAYMENT METHOD: DATE SHIPPED:

PAYMENT DATE: SHIPPING SERVICE:

PROCESS: STARTED   DONE   CANCELED   TRACKING NO.:

ORDER NO.:	NAME:		DATE:	
	CONTACT:		EMAIL:	
	ADDRESS:			

ITEM NO.	ITEM DESCRIPTION	QTY.	PRICE

NOTES:		SUBTOTAL	
		SHIPPING	
		DISCOUNT	
		TOTAL	

PAYMENT METHOD: DATE SHIPPED:

PAYMENT DATE: SHIPPING SERVICE:

PROCESS: STARTED   DONE   CANCELED   TRACKING NO.:

ORDER NO.:	NAME:		DATE:	
	CONTACT:		EMAIL:	
	ADDRESS:			

ITEM NO.	ITEM DESCRIPTION	QTY.	PRICE

NOTES:		SUBTOTAL	
		SHIPPING	
		DISCOUNT	
		TOTAL	

PAYMENT METHOD: DATE SHIPPED:

PAYMENT DATE: SHIPPING SERVICE:

PROCESS: STARTED   DONE   CANCELED   TRACKING NO.:

ORDER NO.:	NAME:		DATE:	
	CONTACT:		EMAIL:	
	ADDRESS:			

ITEM NO.	ITEM DESCRIPTION	QTY.	PRICE

NOTES:		SUBTOTAL	
		SHIPPING	
		DISCOUNT	
		TOTAL	

PAYMENT METHOD: DATE SHIPPED:

PAYMENT DATE: SHIPPING SERVICE:

PROCESS: STARTED   DONE   CANCELED   TRACKING NO.:

ORDER NO.:	NAME:		DATE:	
	CONTACT:		EMAIL:	
	ADDRESS:			

ITEM NO.	ITEM DESCRIPTION	QTY.	PRICE

NOTES:		
	SUBTOTAL	
	SHIPPING	
	DISCOUNT	
	TOTAL	

PAYMENT METHOD: DATE SHIPPED:

PAYMENT DATE: SHIPPING SERVICE:

PROCESS: STARTED   DONE   CANCELED   TRACKING NO.:

ORDER NO.:	NAME:		DATE:	
	CONTACT:		EMAIL:	
	ADDRESS:			

ITEM NO.	ITEM DESCRIPTION	QTY.	PRICE

NOTES:		
	SUBTOTAL	
	SHIPPING	
	DISCOUNT	
	TOTAL	

PAYMENT METHOD: DATE SHIPPED:

PAYMENT DATE: SHIPPING SERVICE:

PROCESS: STARTED   DONE   CANCELED   TRACKING NO.:

ORDER NO.:	NAME:		DATE:	
	CONTACT:		EMAIL:	
	ADDRESS:			

ITEM NO.	ITEM DESCRIPTION	QTY.	PRICE

NOTES:		SUBTOTAL	
		SHIPPING	
		DISCOUNT	
		TOTAL	

PAYMENT METHOD: DATE SHIPPED:

PAYMENT DATE: SHIPPING SERVICE:

PROCESS: STARTED   DONE   CANCELED   TRACKING NO.:

ORDER NO.:	NAME:		DATE:	
	CONTACT:		EMAIL:	
	ADDRESS:			

ITEM NO.	ITEM DESCRIPTION	QTY.	PRICE

NOTES:		SUBTOTAL	
		SHIPPING	
		DISCOUNT	
		TOTAL	

PAYMENT METHOD: DATE SHIPPED:

PAYMENT DATE: SHIPPING SERVICE:

PROCESS: STARTED   DONE   CANCELED   TRACKING NO.:

ORDER NO.:	NAME:		DATE:	
	CONTACT:		EMAIL:	
	ADDRESS:			

ITEM NO.	ITEM DESCRIPTION	QTY.	PRICE

NOTES:		SUBTOTAL	
		SHIPPING	
		DISCOUNT	
		TOTAL	

PAYMENT METHOD: DATE SHIPPED:

PAYMENT DATE: SHIPPING SERVICE:

PROCESS: STARTED   DONE   CANCELED   TRACKING NO.:

ORDER NO.:	NAME:		DATE:	
	CONTACT:		EMAIL:	
	ADDRESS:			

ITEM NO.	ITEM DESCRIPTION	QTY.	PRICE

NOTES:		SUBTOTAL	
		SHIPPING	
		DISCOUNT	
		TOTAL	

PAYMENT METHOD: DATE SHIPPED:

PAYMENT DATE: SHIPPING SERVICE:

PROCESS: STARTED   DONE   CANCELED   TRACKING NO.:

ORDER NO.:	NAME:		DATE:	
	CONTACT:		EMAIL:	
	ADDRESS:			

ITEM NO.	ITEM DESCRIPTION	QTY.	PRICE

NOTES:		
	SUBTOTAL	
	SHIPPING	
	DISCOUNT	
	TOTAL	

PAYMENT METHOD: DATE SHIPPED:

PAYMENT DATE: SHIPPING SERVICE:

PROCESS: STARTED   DONE   CANCELED   TRACKING NO.:

ORDER NO.:	NAME:		DATE:	
	CONTACT:		EMAIL:	
	ADDRESS:			

ITEM NO.	ITEM DESCRIPTION	QTY.	PRICE

NOTES:		
	SUBTOTAL	
	SHIPPING	
	DISCOUNT	
	TOTAL	

PAYMENT METHOD: DATE SHIPPED:

PAYMENT DATE: SHIPPING SERVICE:

PROCESS: STARTED   DONE   CANCELED   TRACKING NO.:

ORDER NO.:	NAME:		DATE:	
	CONTACT:		EMAIL:	
	ADDRESS:			

ITEM NO.	ITEM DESCRIPTION	QTY.	PRICE

NOTES:		
	SUBTOTAL	
	SHIPPING	
	DISCOUNT	
	TOTAL	

PAYMENT METHOD: DATE SHIPPED:

PAYMENT DATE: SHIPPING SERVICE:

PROCESS: STARTED   DONE   CANCELED   TRACKING NO.:

ORDER NO.:	NAME:		DATE:	
	CONTACT:		EMAIL:	
	ADDRESS:			

ITEM NO.	ITEM DESCRIPTION	QTY.	PRICE

NOTES:		
	SUBTOTAL	
	SHIPPING	
	DISCOUNT	
	TOTAL	

PAYMENT METHOD: DATE SHIPPED:

PAYMENT DATE: SHIPPING SERVICE:

PROCESS: STARTED   DONE   CANCELED   TRACKING NO.:

ORDER NO.:	NAME:		DATE:	
	CONTACT:		EMAIL:	
	ADDRESS:			

ITEM NO.	ITEM DESCRIPTION	QTY.	PRICE

NOTES:		SUBTOTAL	
		SHIPPING	
		DISCOUNT	
		TOTAL	

PAYMENT METHOD: DATE SHIPPED:

PAYMENT DATE: SHIPPING SERVICE:

PROCESS: STARTED   DONE   CANCELED   TRACKING NO.:

ORDER NO.:	NAME:		DATE:	
	CONTACT:		EMAIL:	
	ADDRESS:			

ITEM NO.	ITEM DESCRIPTION	QTY.	PRICE

NOTES:		SUBTOTAL	
		SHIPPING	
		DISCOUNT	
		TOTAL	

PAYMENT METHOD: DATE SHIPPED:

PAYMENT DATE: SHIPPING SERVICE:

PROCESS: STARTED   DONE   CANCELED   TRACKING NO.:

ORDER NO.:	NAME:		DATE:	
	CONTACT:		EMAIL:	
	ADDRESS:			

ITEM NO.	ITEM DESCRIPTION	QTY.	PRICE

NOTES:		
	SUBTOTAL	
	SHIPPING	
	DISCOUNT	
	TOTAL	

PAYMENT METHOD: DATE SHIPPED:

PAYMENT DATE: SHIPPING SERVICE:

PROCESS: STARTED   DONE   CANCELED   TRACKING NO.:

ORDER NO.:	NAME:		DATE:	
	CONTACT:		EMAIL:	
	ADDRESS:			

ITEM NO.	ITEM DESCRIPTION	QTY.	PRICE

NOTES:		
	SUBTOTAL	
	SHIPPING	
	DISCOUNT	
	TOTAL	

PAYMENT METHOD: DATE SHIPPED:

PAYMENT DATE: SHIPPING SERVICE:

PROCESS: STARTED   DONE   CANCELED   TRACKING NO.:

ORDER NO.:	NAME:		DATE:	
	CONTACT:		EMAIL:	
	ADDRESS:			

ITEM NO.	ITEM DESCRIPTION	QTY.	PRICE

NOTES:		
	SUBTOTAL	
	SHIPPING	
	DISCOUNT	
	TOTAL	

PAYMENT METHOD: DATE SHIPPED:

PAYMENT DATE: SHIPPING SERVICE:

PROCESS: STARTED   DONE   CANCELED   TRACKING NO.:

ORDER NO.:	NAME:		DATE:	
	CONTACT:		EMAIL:	
	ADDRESS:			

ITEM NO.	ITEM DESCRIPTION	QTY.	PRICE

NOTES:		
	SUBTOTAL	
	SHIPPING	
	DISCOUNT	
	TOTAL	

PAYMENT METHOD: DATE SHIPPED:

PAYMENT DATE: SHIPPING SERVICE:

PROCESS: STARTED   DONE   CANCELED   TRACKING NO.:

ORDER NO.:	NAME:		DATE:	
	CONTACT:		EMAIL:	
	ADDRESS:			

ITEM NO.	ITEM DESCRIPTION	QTY.	PRICE

NOTES:		SUBTOTAL	
		SHIPPING	
		DISCOUNT	
		TOTAL	

PAYMENT METHOD: DATE SHIPPED:

PAYMENT DATE: SHIPPING SERVICE:

PROCESS: STARTED   DONE   CANCELED   TRACKING NO.:

ORDER NO.:	NAME:		DATE:	
	CONTACT:		EMAIL:	
	ADDRESS:			

ITEM NO.	ITEM DESCRIPTION	QTY.	PRICE

NOTES:		SUBTOTAL	
		SHIPPING	
		DISCOUNT	
		TOTAL	

PAYMENT METHOD: DATE SHIPPED:

PAYMENT DATE: SHIPPING SERVICE:

PROCESS: STARTED   DONE   CANCELED   TRACKING NO.:

ORDER NO.:	NAME:		DATE:	
	CONTACT:		EMAIL:	
	ADDRESS:			

ITEM NO.	ITEM DESCRIPTION	QTY.	PRICE

NOTES:		SUBTOTAL	
		SHIPPING	
		DISCOUNT	
		TOTAL	

PAYMENT METHOD: DATE SHIPPED:

PAYMENT DATE: SHIPPING SERVICE:

PROCESS: STARTED   DONE   CANCELED   TRACKING NO.:

ORDER NO.:	NAME:		DATE:	
	CONTACT:		EMAIL:	
	ADDRESS:			

ITEM NO.	ITEM DESCRIPTION	QTY.	PRICE

NOTES:		SUBTOTAL	
		SHIPPING	
		DISCOUNT	
		TOTAL	

PAYMENT METHOD: DATE SHIPPED:

PAYMENT DATE: SHIPPING SERVICE:

PROCESS: STARTED   DONE   CANCELED   TRACKING NO.:

ORDER NO.:	NAME:		DATE:	
	CONTACT:		EMAIL:	
	ADDRESS:			

ITEM NO.	ITEM DESCRIPTION	QTY.	PRICE

NOTES:	SUBTOTAL	
	SHIPPING	
	DISCOUNT	
	TOTAL	

PAYMENT METHOD: DATE SHIPPED:

PAYMENT DATE: SHIPPING SERVICE:

PROCESS: STARTED   DONE   CANCELED   TRACKING NO.:

ORDER NO.:	NAME:		DATE:	
	CONTACT:		EMAIL:	
	ADDRESS:			

ITEM NO.	ITEM DESCRIPTION	QTY.	PRICE

NOTES:	SUBTOTAL	
	SHIPPING	
	DISCOUNT	
	TOTAL	

PAYMENT METHOD: DATE SHIPPED:

PAYMENT DATE: SHIPPING SERVICE:

PROCESS: STARTED   DONE   CANCELED   TRACKING NO.:

ORDER NO.:	NAME:		DATE:	
	CONTACT:		EMAIL:	
	ADDRESS:			

ITEM NO.	ITEM DESCRIPTION	QTY.	PRICE

NOTES:			
	SUBTOTAL		
	SHIPPING		
	DISCOUNT		
	TOTAL		

PAYMENT METHOD: DATE SHIPPED:

PAYMENT DATE: SHIPPING SERVICE:

PROCESS: STARTED   DONE   CANCELED   TRACKING NO.:

ORDER NO.:	NAME:		DATE:	
	CONTACT:		EMAIL:	
	ADDRESS:			

ITEM NO.	ITEM DESCRIPTION	QTY.	PRICE

NOTES:			
	SUBTOTAL		
	SHIPPING		
	DISCOUNT		
	TOTAL		

PAYMENT METHOD: DATE SHIPPED:

PAYMENT DATE: SHIPPING SERVICE:

PROCESS: STARTED   DONE   CANCELED   TRACKING NO.:

ORDER NO.:	NAME:		DATE:	
	CONTACT:		EMAIL:	
	ADDRESS:			

ITEM NO.	ITEM DESCRIPTION	QTY.	PRICE

NOTES:		SUBTOTAL	
		SHIPPING	
		DISCOUNT	
		TOTAL	

PAYMENT METHOD: DATE SHIPPED:

PAYMENT DATE: SHIPPING SERVICE:

PROCESS: ☐ STARTED ☐ DONE ☐ CANCELED   TRACKING NO.:

ORDER NO.:	NAME:		DATE:	
	CONTACT:		EMAIL:	
	ADDRESS:			

ITEM NO.	ITEM DESCRIPTION	QTY.	PRICE

NOTES:		SUBTOTAL	
		SHIPPING	
		DISCOUNT	
		TOTAL	

PAYMENT METHOD: DATE SHIPPED:

PAYMENT DATE: SHIPPING SERVICE:

PROCESS: ☐ STARTED ☐ DONE ☐ CANCELED   TRACKING NO.:

ORDER NO.:	NAME:		DATE:	
	CONTACT:		EMAIL:	
	ADDRESS:			

ITEM NO.	ITEM DESCRIPTION	QTY.	PRICE

NOTES:		SUBTOTAL	
		SHIPPING	
		DISCOUNT	
		TOTAL	

PAYMENT METHOD: DATE SHIPPED:

PAYMENT DATE: SHIPPING SERVICE:

PROCESS: STARTED   DONE   CANCELED   TRACKING NO.:

ORDER NO.:	NAME:		DATE:	
	CONTACT:		EMAIL:	
	ADDRESS:			

ITEM NO.	ITEM DESCRIPTION	QTY.	PRICE

NOTES:		SUBTOTAL	
		SHIPPING	
		DISCOUNT	
		TOTAL	

PAYMENT METHOD: DATE SHIPPED:

PAYMENT DATE: SHIPPING SERVICE:

PROCESS: STARTED   DONE   CANCELED   TRACKING NO.:

ORDER NO.:	NAME:		DATE:	
	CONTACT:		EMAIL:	
	ADDRESS:			

ITEM NO.	ITEM DESCRIPTION	QTY.	PRICE

NOTES:		
	SUBTOTAL	
	SHIPPING	
	DISCOUNT	
	TOTAL	

PAYMENT METHOD: DATE SHIPPED:

PAYMENT DATE: SHIPPING SERVICE:

PROCESS: STARTED   DONE   CANCELED   TRACKING NO.:

ORDER NO.:	NAME:		DATE:	
	CONTACT:		EMAIL:	
	ADDRESS:			

ITEM NO.	ITEM DESCRIPTION	QTY.	PRICE

NOTES:		
	SUBTOTAL	
	SHIPPING	
	DISCOUNT	
	TOTAL	

PAYMENT METHOD: DATE SHIPPED:

PAYMENT DATE: SHIPPING SERVICE:

PROCESS: STARTED   DONE   CANCELED   TRACKING NO.:

ORDER NO.:	NAME:		DATE:	
	CONTACT:		EMAIL:	
	ADDRESS:			

ITEM NO.	ITEM DESCRIPTION	QTY.	PRICE

NOTES:		
	SUBTOTAL	
	SHIPPING	
	DISCOUNT	
	TOTAL	

PAYMENT METHOD: DATE SHIPPED:

PAYMENT DATE: SHIPPING SERVICE:

PROCESS: STARTED   DONE   CANCELED   TRACKING NO.:

ORDER NO.:	NAME:		DATE:	
	CONTACT:		EMAIL:	
	ADDRESS:			

ITEM NO.	ITEM DESCRIPTION	QTY.	PRICE

NOTES:		
	SUBTOTAL	
	SHIPPING	
	DISCOUNT	
	TOTAL	

PAYMENT METHOD: DATE SHIPPED:

PAYMENT DATE: SHIPPING SERVICE:

PROCESS: STARTED   DONE   CANCELED   TRACKING NO.:

ORDER NO.:	NAME:			DATE:	
	CONTACT:			EMAIL:	
	ADDRESS:				

ITEM NO.	ITEM DESCRIPTION	QTY.	PRICE

NOTES:			
		SUBTOTAL	
		SHIPPING	
		DISCOUNT	
		TOTAL	

PAYMENT METHOD: DATE SHIPPED:

PAYMENT DATE: SHIPPING SERVICE:

PROCESS: STARTED DONE CANCELED TRACKING NO.:

ORDER NO.:	NAME:			DATE:	
	CONTACT:			EMAIL:	
	ADDRESS:				

ITEM NO.	ITEM DESCRIPTION	QTY.	PRICE

NOTES:			
		SUBTOTAL	
		SHIPPING	
		DISCOUNT	
		TOTAL	

PAYMENT METHOD: DATE SHIPPED:

PAYMENT DATE: SHIPPING SERVICE:

PROCESS: STARTED DONE CANCELED TRACKING NO.:

ORDER NO.:	NAME:		DATE:	
	CONTACT:		EMAIL:	
	ADDRESS:			

ITEM NO.	ITEM DESCRIPTION	QTY.	PRICE

NOTES:	SUBTOTAL	
	SHIPPING	
	DISCOUNT	
	TOTAL	

PAYMENT METHOD: DATE SHIPPED:

PAYMENT DATE: SHIPPING SERVICE:

PROCESS: STARTED   DONE   CANCELED   TRACKING NO.:

ORDER NO.:	NAME:		DATE:	
	CONTACT:		EMAIL:	
	ADDRESS:			

ITEM NO.	ITEM DESCRIPTION	QTY.	PRICE

NOTES:	SUBTOTAL	
	SHIPPING	
	DISCOUNT	
	TOTAL	

PAYMENT METHOD: DATE SHIPPED:

PAYMENT DATE: SHIPPING SERVICE:

PROCESS: STARTED   DONE   CANCELED   TRACKING NO.:

ORDER NO.:	NAME:		DATE:	
	CONTACT:		EMAIL:	
	ADDRESS:			

ITEM NO.	ITEM DESCRIPTION	QTY.	PRICE

NOTES:		
	SUBTOTAL	
	SHIPPING	
	DISCOUNT	
	TOTAL	

PAYMENT METHOD: DATE SHIPPED:

PAYMENT DATE: SHIPPING SERVICE:

PROCESS: STARTED DONE CANCELED TRACKING NO.:

ORDER NO.:	NAME:		DATE:	
	CONTACT:		EMAIL:	
	ADDRESS:			

ITEM NO.	ITEM DESCRIPTION	QTY.	PRICE

NOTES:		
	SUBTOTAL	
	SHIPPING	
	DISCOUNT	
	TOTAL	

PAYMENT METHOD: DATE SHIPPED:

PAYMENT DATE: SHIPPING SERVICE:

PROCESS: STARTED DONE CANCELED TRACKING NO.:

ORDER NO.:	NAME:			DATE:	
	CONTACT:			EMAIL:	
	ADDRESS:				

ITEM NO.	ITEM DESCRIPTION	QTY.	PRICE

NOTES:		SUBTOTAL	
		SHIPPING	
		DISCOUNT	
		TOTAL	

PAYMENT METHOD: DATE SHIPPED:

PAYMENT DATE: SHIPPING SERVICE:

PROCESS: STARTED DONE CANCELED TRACKING NO.:

ORDER NO.:	NAME:			DATE:	
	CONTACT:			EMAIL:	
	ADDRESS:				

ITEM NO.	ITEM DESCRIPTION	QTY.	PRICE

NOTES:		SUBTOTAL	
		SHIPPING	
		DISCOUNT	
		TOTAL	

PAYMENT METHOD: DATE SHIPPED:

PAYMENT DATE: SHIPPING SERVICE:

PROCESS: STARTED DONE CANCELED TRACKING NO.:

ORDER NO.:	NAME:		DATE:	
	CONTACT:		EMAIL:	
	ADDRESS:			

ITEM NO.	ITEM DESCRIPTION	QTY.	PRICE

NOTES:		
	SUBTOTAL	
	SHIPPING	
	DISCOUNT	
	TOTAL	

PAYMENT METHOD: DATE SHIPPED:

PAYMENT DATE: SHIPPING SERVICE:

PROCESS: STARTED   DONE   CANCELED   TRACKING NO.:

ORDER NO.:	NAME:		DATE:	
	CONTACT:		EMAIL:	
	ADDRESS:			

ITEM NO.	ITEM DESCRIPTION	QTY.	PRICE

NOTES:		
	SUBTOTAL	
	SHIPPING	
	DISCOUNT	
	TOTAL	

PAYMENT METHOD: DATE SHIPPED:

PAYMENT DATE: SHIPPING SERVICE:

PROCESS: STARTED   DONE   CANCELED   TRACKING NO.:

ORDER NO.:	NAME:		DATE:	
	CONTACT:		EMAIL:	
	ADDRESS:			

ITEM NO.	ITEM DESCRIPTION	QTY.	PRICE

NOTES:		SUBTOTAL	
		SHIPPING	
		DISCOUNT	
		TOTAL	

PAYMENT METHOD: DATE SHIPPED:

PAYMENT DATE: SHIPPING SERVICE:

PROCESS: STARTED   DONE   CANCELED   TRACKING NO.:

ORDER NO.:	NAME:		DATE:	
	CONTACT:		EMAIL:	
	ADDRESS:			

ITEM NO.	ITEM DESCRIPTION	QTY.	PRICE

NOTES:		SUBTOTAL	
		SHIPPING	
		DISCOUNT	
		TOTAL	

PAYMENT METHOD: DATE SHIPPED:

PAYMENT DATE: SHIPPING SERVICE:

PROCESS: STARTED   DONE   CANCELED   TRACKING NO.:

ORDER NO.:	NAME:			DATE:	
	CONTACT:			EMAIL:	
	ADDRESS:				
ITEM NO.	ITEM DESCRIPTION			QTY.	PRICE
NOTES:				SUBTOTAL	
				SHIPPING	
				DISCOUNT	
				TOTAL	

PAYMENT METHOD: DATE SHIPPED:

PAYMENT DATE: SHIPPING SERVICE:

PROCESS: STARTED   DONE   CANCELED   TRACKING NO.:

ORDER NO.:	NAME:			DATE:	
	CONTACT:			EMAIL:	
	ADDRESS:				
ITEM NO.	ITEM DESCRIPTION			QTY.	PRICE
NOTES:				SUBTOTAL	
				SHIPPING	
				DISCOUNT	
				TOTAL	

PAYMENT METHOD: DATE SHIPPED:

PAYMENT DATE: SHIPPING SERVICE:

PROCESS: STARTED   DONE   CANCELED   TRACKING NO.:

ORDER NO.:	NAME:		DATE:	
	CONTACT:		EMAIL:	
	ADDRESS:			

ITEM NO.	ITEM DESCRIPTION	QTY.	PRICE

NOTES:		
	SUBTOTAL	
	SHIPPING	
	DISCOUNT	
	TOTAL	

PAYMENT METHOD: DATE SHIPPED:

PAYMENT DATE: SHIPPING SERVICE:

PROCESS: STARTED   DONE   CANCELED   **TRACKING NO.:**

ORDER NO.:	NAME:		DATE:	
	CONTACT:		EMAIL:	
	ADDRESS:			

ITEM NO.	ITEM DESCRIPTION	QTY.	PRICE

NOTES:		
	SUBTOTAL	
	SHIPPING	
	DISCOUNT	
	TOTAL	

PAYMENT METHOD: DATE SHIPPED:

PAYMENT DATE: SHIPPING SERVICE:

PROCESS: STARTED   DONE   CANCELED   **TRACKING NO.:**

ORDER NO.:	NAME:		DATE:	
	CONTACT:		EMAIL:	
	ADDRESS:			

ITEM NO.	ITEM DESCRIPTION	QTY.	PRICE

NOTES:		
	SUBTOTAL	
	SHIPPING	
	DISCOUNT	
	TOTAL	

PAYMENT METHOD: DATE SHIPPED:

PAYMENT DATE: SHIPPING SERVICE:

PROCESS: STARTED   DONE   CANCELED   TRACKING NO.:

ORDER NO.:	NAME:		DATE:	
	CONTACT:		EMAIL:	
	ADDRESS:			

ITEM NO.	ITEM DESCRIPTION	QTY.	PRICE

NOTES:		
	SUBTOTAL	
	SHIPPING	
	DISCOUNT	
	TOTAL	

PAYMENT METHOD: DATE SHIPPED:

PAYMENT DATE: SHIPPING SERVICE:

PROCESS: STARTED   DONE   CANCELED   TRACKING NO.:

ORDER NO.:	NAME:		DATE:	
	CONTACT:		EMAIL:	
	ADDRESS:			

ITEM NO.	ITEM DESCRIPTION	QTY.	PRICE

NOTES:		SUBTOTAL	
		SHIPPING	
		DISCOUNT	
		TOTAL	

PAYMENT METHOD: DATE SHIPPED:

PAYMENT DATE: SHIPPING SERVICE:

PROCESS: STARTED   DONE   CANCELED   TRACKING NO.:

ORDER NO.:	NAME:		DATE:	
	CONTACT:		EMAIL:	
	ADDRESS:			

ITEM NO.	ITEM DESCRIPTION	QTY.	PRICE

NOTES:		SUBTOTAL	
		SHIPPING	
		DISCOUNT	
		TOTAL	

PAYMENT METHOD: DATE SHIPPED:

PAYMENT DATE: SHIPPING SERVICE:

PROCESS: STARTED   DONE   CANCELED   TRACKING NO.:

ORDER NO.:	NAME:			DATE:	
	CONTACT:			EMAIL:	
	ADDRESS:				

ITEM NO.	ITEM DESCRIPTION	QTY.	PRICE

NOTES:		
	SUBTOTAL	
	SHIPPING	
	DISCOUNT	
	TOTAL	

PAYMENT METHOD: DATE SHIPPED:

PAYMENT DATE: SHIPPING SERVICE:

PROCESS: STARTED   DONE   CANCELED   TRACKING NO.:

ORDER NO.:	NAME:			DATE:	
	CONTACT:			EMAIL:	
	ADDRESS:				

ITEM NO.	ITEM DESCRIPTION	QTY.	PRICE

NOTES:		
	SUBTOTAL	
	SHIPPING	
	DISCOUNT	
	TOTAL	

PAYMENT METHOD: DATE SHIPPED:

PAYMENT DATE: SHIPPING SERVICE:

PROCESS: STARTED   DONE   CANCELED   TRACKING NO.:

Made in the USA
Las Vegas, NV
27 December 2024

15456395R10063